Mastering Social Media:

The Blueprint to Online Success. Build your Media team, Harness AI tools, and Free your Time.

I0454468

By William Thadius Stewart

Dedication:

To my cherished wife, Nikolett Stewart,

Every word inked in this book has been inspired by the love, patience, and unwavering belief you've showered upon me. As I sat for countless hours, pouring my soul onto these pages, it was your gentle encouragement and faith that spurred me on. You have witnessed my lows, celebrated my highs, and held my hand through the winding path of this journey.

Your strength has been my beacon, guiding me away from past vices and illuminating the path towards my dreams. Without you, the idea of becoming a laptop millionaire would have remained a fleeting thought, and this book would never have graced the hands of countless readers.

Every time I glance over at the dedication sections in books, I now truly comprehend the depth of gratitude and love they represent. I am immeasurably blessed to have you by my side, not just as my partner in life but as my muse, my anchor, and my eternal flame.

This book, while it may bear my name, is as much yours as it is mine. It stands as a tribute to our shared journey, our challenges, our triumphs, and the unyielding power of our love.

Thank you, Nikolett, for being my guiding star, my anchor, and the very essence of my existence. Without you, this dream would never have been realized.

Goal of This Book

In the vast and often overwhelming realm of social media, one universal truth remains: the first step is often the hardest. Overcoming the inertia of starting can be a formidable challenge, especially when faced with an avalanche of tasks like content creation, editing, and consistent posting. This book aims to not only guide you through that initial leap but also simplify the subsequent steps of your journey.

The intention behind these pages is simple:

- **Demystify** the complexities of social media.
- **Streamline** the content creation process.
- **Empower** you to delegate, automate, and optimize every aspect of your social media presence.

By the end of this guide, you'll gain a solid understanding of your game plan, a clear vision of the roles you'll need to fill (or outsource), and the freedom to focus solely on your primary task: producing raw content. Everything else? It's handled.

Let's dive into the three powerful tools this book promises to arm you with:

- **Edit Without Editing:** Unearth the magic of AI and automated tools that revolutionize the editing process. You'll be able to deliver high-quality content without spending hours on tedious edits.
- **Scheduled & Autonomous Posting:** Discover the wonders of platform management tools and the art of delegation. Learn how you can have content regularly posted across various platforms, even without lifting a finger. With the right strategies and team members in place, you might never have to hit the 'post' button again!
- **Your AI Starter Kit:** Whether you're delving into video

creation, graphic design, or any other realm of content, this toolkit will introduce you to the essential AI tools. They're designed to simplify tasks, optimize your processes, and elevate the quality of your output.

In essence, this book is about liberating you from the shackles of time-consuming tasks and giving you the freedom to create without constraints. Bid farewell to long editing hours, say goodbye to the need for exhaustive planning, and embrace a future where you're not in it alone.
Let's embark on this journey together. I'm excited to show you the way.

Preface: For the Straight Shooters

To the ones who value time as their most precious commodity, who dive head-first into action without the need for lengthy intros and exhaustive explanations, I see you. I've written many pages in this book, diving deep into the intricacies of the digital world, but I understand that some of you are here for the essence, the distilled wisdom—the meat without the bones.

If you're one of those digital entrepreneurs (or soon-to-be) who's saying, "Just give me the game plan," then I've got you covered. The conclusion of this book is designed precisely for you. It strips away the layers and offers a straight-to-the-point, actionable toolkit for your social media journey.

Of course, I'd love for you to immerse yourself in the entirety of the content, to savor each chapter and anecdote. But I respect the hustle, the urgency, and the desire for immediate action. So, if you're itching to get started, skip to the conclusion, grab the tools, and sprint ahead.

For those ready to take the scenic route, buckle up. We're diving deep into the world of social media, exploring every nook and cranny. Whichever path you choose, know that this book has something invaluable for you.

Here's to your journey, fast or slow, but always forward.

TABLE OF CONTENTS:

Chapter 1: The Social Media Revolution

In today's world, social media isn't a mere platform—it's the epicenter of connectivity, commerce, and community.

Section 1.1: The New Era of Engagement

Gone are the days of cold calls and door knocking. The power to reach a global audience is at our fingertips. With just a single post, you can engage thousands. And, with the right strategy, one viral moment can transform your brand forever.

Subsection 1.1.1: The Massive Scale of Impact

Think about the sheer scale: one video can have over a million eyes on it. The reach and power of social media dwarf traditional forms of communication. It's not about replacing the old ways, but enhancing your approach with this powerful tool.

Section 1.2: Creating Content Effortlessly

The age-old myth is that good content requires hours of hard work. Not anymore. With tools like Mojo and Opus.pro, top-tier content creation is just a few clicks away.

Subsection 1.2.1: The Magic of Opus.pro

This isn't just another editing software. Opus.pro offers a whopping 120 free minutes of footage editing. That's 120 potential videos waiting to be made. For talkative content, podcasts, or any spoken word pieces, Opus.pro is your go-to.

Subsection 1.2.2: Mojo: For the Silent Artistry

When words aren't needed, let the visuals do the talking. Mojo's aesthetic-driven templates are perfect for crafting visually compelling stories without uttering a single word.

Section 1.3: Elevate with Enhanced Captions

With THE CAPTIONs app, your content gets the finishing touches it deserves. No longer are captions an afterthought; they're an integral part of your content narrative.

Section 1.4: The Power of Automation

Maximize productivity by letting ChatGPT handle the routine. Focus on the bigger picture while ChatGPT takes care of the nuances.

Chapter 2: Future-Proofing: The Evolving Landscape of Social Media

The digital age is a tapestry of constant evolution. Stay ahead, anticipate trends, and be prepared to pivot as the winds of change blow.

Section 5.1: Trends on the Horizon

From augmented reality to AI-driven content, explore the innovations that are set to redefine social media.

Subsection 5.1.1: The Rise of Virtual Personalities

Synthesia AI and the dawn of virtual avatars. Understand how they'll shape content creation in the near future.

Subsection 5.1.2: The Ever-Changing Algorithm

Mastering the algorithm today doesn't guarantee success tomorrow. Develop adaptive strategies to stay on top.

Section 5.2: Sustainability in the Digital Age

It's not about fleeting success; it's about building a lasting legacy. Dive into practices that ensure your brand thrives, now and always.

Chapter 3: Monetizing Your Online Presence

With the right strategies, your passion can become your paycheck. Discover the diverse avenues to translate your digital influence into tangible gains.

Section 6.1: Beyond Ad Revenue

While ad revenue is a consistent earner, it's just the tip of the iceberg. Dive deeper into the plethora of monetization options available.

Subsection 6.1.1: Affiliate Marketing Magic

Promote products, earn commissions. Learn the ins and outs of affiliate marketing and find the best fit for your brand.

Subsection 6.1.2: Selling Merchandise & Products

Turn your brand into a household name. From T-shirts to custom merchandise, discover how to bring your brand to physical form.

Section 6.2: Leveraging Connections

It's not just about what you know but who you know. Unlock the potential of partnerships, collaborations, and sponsorships.

Subsection 6.2.1: The Power of Sponsorships

Big brands are always on the lookout for influencers to amplify their message. Find out how to position yourself as the ideal partner.

Subsection 6.2.2: Paid Partnerships & Collaborations

Team up with fellow influencers for win-win scenarios. Learn how to craft the perfect pitch and negotiate deals that benefit all parties involved.

Chapter 4: Pitching The Game-Changer: ChatGPT

The future of content creation is here, and its name is ChatGPT. Explore how this AI tool can revolutionize your content strategy for just $20 a month.

Section 7.1: Beyond Basic Text

ChatGPT isn't just a text tool. It's a multifaceted platform ready to amplify your online presence.

Subsection 7.1.1: Content Ideas & Brainstorming

Stuck in a creative rut? Let ChatGPT be your muse, suggesting fresh content ideas tailored to your niche.

Subsection 7.1.2: Brand Refinement & Positioning

Clarify your brand voice and positioning with AI-guided strategies. Stand out in a crowded online marketplace.

Section 7.2: The Art of Engagement

Engaging with your audience has never been easier. From crafting compelling captions to replying to comments, ChatGPT has your back.

Subsection 7.2.1: Crafting Captivating Captions

Say goodbye to bland and generic captions. Discover how to craft compelling narratives that resonate with your audience.

Subsection 7.2.2: Bio Optimization & First Impressions

Your bio is your brand's digital handshake. Learn how to make a lasting impression and draw followers into your world.

Chapter 5: Staying Ahead: Continuous Learning & Adaptation

In the fast-paced world of social media, complacency is your biggest foe. Stay hungry, stay curious, and always be ready to adapt.

Section 8.1: The Importance of Continuous Education

The digital landscape is ever-evolving. Understand the importance of continuous learning to stay relevant.

Subsection 8.1.1: Platforms & Tools

From emerging social platforms to innovative content tools, stay updated with the latest in the industry.

Subsection 8.1.2: Adapting to Algorithm Changes

The only constant in the world of social media algorithms is change. Develop a proactive approach to navigate these shifts seamlessly.

Section 8.2: Seeking Inspiration Outside Your Niche

Sometimes, the best ideas come from unexpected places. Cultivate the habit of seeking inspiration outside your niche and bringing fresh perspectives to your content.

Chapter 6: Networking & Collaboration

Every influencer's journey is intertwined with countless others. Your network is your net worth in the world of social media.

Section 9.1: The Power of Connections

Don't underestimate the power of a simple message or comment. The doors of collaboration are often just a click away.

Subsection 9.1.1: Reaching Out to Like-Minded Creators

Collaboration over competition is the mantra. Explore ways to identify and connect with potential partners in content creation.

Subsection 9.1.2: Building Mutually Beneficial Relationships

Forge partnerships where both parties grow and thrive. Understand the art of negotiation and building win-win scenarios.

Section 9.2: Handling Outreach

As your profile grows, so will the number of pitches and outreach messages. Navigate this influx with grace and efficiency.

Subsection 9.2.1: Vetting Opportunities

Not all that glitters is gold. Develop a keen sense for vetting collaboration opportunities and discerning genuine offers from time-wasters.

Subsection 9.2.2: Establishing Boundaries
Your time and energy are precious. Learn to set clear boundaries and prioritize collaborations that align with your brand and values.

Chapter 7: Handling Feedback & Trolls
Every public figure has critics. Transform criticism into growth opportunities and learn to deal with the unavoidable trolls.

Section 10.1: Constructive Criticism vs. Trolling
There's a thin line between genuine feedback and mindless trolling. Learn to distinguish the two and respond accordingly.

Subsection 10.1.1: Embracing Constructive Feedback
Feedback is a gift. Understand the importance of self-reflection and continuous improvement based on genuine critiques.

Subsection 10.1.2: "Those who mind don't matter, and those who matter don't mind."
Remember this mantra when dealing with trolls. Your focus should always be on those who genuinely support and appreciate your work.

Section 10.2: Using AI for Handling Feedback

In an age of AI, let tools like ChatGPT be your ally in managing feedback efficiently.

Subsection 10.2.1: Crafting Thoughtful Responses

No more agonizing over the perfect response. Use AI to craft thoughtful and appropriate replies, even to the toughest critiques.

Subsection 10.2.2: Automating Feedback Management

Time is of the essence. Explore ways to automate feedback management without losing the personal touch.

Chapter 8: The Future of Social Media

As we look to the horizon, the digital landscape continues to evolve. Stay prepared for the future and the shifts it brings.

Section 11.1: Emerging Platforms & Trends

Stay ahead of the curve. Keep an eye out for the next big thing in social media.

Subsection 11.1.1: Platform Diversification

Don't put all your eggs in one basket. Understand the importance of having a presence across multiple platforms.

Subsection 11.1.2: Staying Updated

The world of social media moves fast. Develop habits and routines to stay updated with the latest trends and shifts.

Section 11.2: Preparing for the Unpredictable

The future is uncertain, but preparation can give you an edge.

Subsection 11.2.1: The Importance of Flexibility

Learn to pivot. Adaptability is a key trait for any successful influencer.

Subsection 11.2.2: Lifelong Learning

The learning never stops. Commit to a journey of continuous growth and self-improvement.

Chapter 9: Monetization & Building a Sustainable Income

Turn your passion into a profession. Social media isn't just about likes and shares; it's a viable income stream if approached strategically.

Section 12.1: Affiliate Marketing & Partnerships

Unlock passive income and establish mutually beneficial business relationships.

Subsection 12.1.1: Identifying the Right Affiliates

Not all affiliate programs are created equal. Pinpoint those that align with your brand and values.

Subsection 12.1.2: Ethical Promotion

Trust is currency. Always promote products and services you genuinely believe in.

Section 12.2: Merchandising & Product Launches

Take your brand to the next level by creating tangible goods or services for your audience.

Subsection 12.2.1: Designing with Your Audience in Mind

Craft products or services that resonate with your followers, turning them into loyal customers.

Subsection 12.2.2: Launch Strategies

Timing is everything. Learn the art of product launches to maximize impact and sales.

Section 12.3: Premium Content & Subscription Models

Reward your most loyal followers with exclusive content, turning your platform into a recurring revenue stream.

Subsection 12.3.1: Choosing the Right Model

Whether it's Patreon, OnlyFans, or YouTube Premium, select the model that fits best with your content strategy.

Subsection 12.3.2: Delivering Value

Your premium content should always feel like a step above. Consistently deliver value to keep your subscribers engaged and satisfied.

Chapter 10: The Long Game: Building a Legacy

It's not just about fleeting fame; it's about establishing a lasting impact and legacy.

Section 13.1: Evolving with the Times

Stay relevant by continually adapting to the ever-changing digital landscape.

Subsection 13.1.1: Lifelong Learning & Adaptation

Commit to a continuous learning journey. Embrace change and adapt accordingly.

Subsection 13.1.2: Legacy Content

Identify and create evergreen content that stands the test of time, acting as a pillar for your brand.

Section 13.2: Planning for the Future

Think beyond the now. Plan for the next phases of your digital career.

Subsection 13.2.1: Succession & Continuity

Who will take the reins when you decide to step back? Think about the long-term continuity of your brand.

Subsection 13.2.2: Expanding Beyond Social Media

Consider other ventures – be it podcasts, movies, or business endeavors. Diversify your impact and sources of income.

Conclusion

Social media mastery is a journey, not a destination. By following this guide and staying true to your authentic self, you're poised to not only achieve digital stardom but also leave a lasting legacy. Remember to always learn, adapt, and evolve. The digital realm waits for no one, but with preparation and passion, you can ride the wave to unprecedented success.

Beginning:

Chapter 1: The Social Media Revolution

Section 1.1: The New Era of Engagement

In today's digital cosmos, the buzzing chatter of countless voices can seem overwhelming. The thought alone can be enough to deter many. Remember when reaching out meant tirelessly walking door to door or cold calling until your voice grew hoarse? Those methods, while noble, are fading into the past. Instead, we find ourselves on the cusp of an era where a single, carefully crafted message can ripple through continents, igniting conversations and sparking connections.

However, the caveat is clear: with the power of global influence comes an unparalleled level of competition. Every tweet, post, or video exists in a universe flooded with content. Yet, it's not the loudest voice that always wins, but the most authentic, strategic, and sometimes, the most technologically adept.

Consider Sarah. Just a few years ago, she was a local artisan, her crafts adorning only a few homes in her neighborhood. The online world seemed daunting, a realm where giants played. But, with a nudge from her niece, she made her debut with a simple video showcasing her craft. As her hands weaved magic, the world watched, shared, and ordered. Today, pieces of her artistry sit in homes from Toronto to Tokyo. Every notification is not just an order but a testament to the global connections she's fostered.

Subsection 1.1.1: The Massive Scale of Impact

The digital universe we navigate daily is vast and unending. It's a place where creativity meets scale. But the massive scale can sometimes feel like an intimidating ocean where your small boat risks being lost among the waves. The challenge isn't just about creating; it's about being seen and heard in a sea of content.

Yet, this vastness is a double-edged sword. While it amplifies the competition, it also magnifies the potential. With the right tools and strategies, your voice can echo across this vast expanse, touching hearts and minds on a scale previously unimagined. It's about not only integrating the tried-and-true methods but also harnessing the unmatched prowess of social media platforms.

James, a teacher from a small town, often reminisced about the stories his grandmother narrated. To preserve these tales, he began sharing them on social media. His humble town stories began to resonate with people from bustling cities to tranquil hamlets. It was a testament that in this expansive digital realm, even the most intimate stories find their audience.

Section 1.2: Creating Content Effortlessly
There's a prevalent myth whispered in the corridors of content creation: Quality takes time. And money. A lot of it. There's an ounce of truth to it. But in an era of technological marvels, the rules are changing rapidly. The dread of investing countless hours, coupled with the fear of burning through savings, holds many potential creators back.

Enter tools like Mojo and Opus.pro. The magic lies not just in their affordability but in

their ability to democratize content creation.
What once required a dedicated team,
expensive equipment, and extensive know-
how is now condensed into intuitive
platforms that offer top-tier results at a
fraction of the cost and time.

Emily, a budding entrepreneur, knew her
startup's story was powerful. Yet, without a
big budget, she struggled to share it. Then
she discovered Opus.pro. Taking her raw
recordings, within minutes, she had a
compelling video. That single video, made
on a shoestring budget, propelled her startup
into the limelight, drawing investors and
customers alike.

Subsection 1.2.2: Mojo: More Than Just Templates

In the visually driven world of today, crafting
your narrative isn't just about the words you
speak; it's equally about the visual tapestry
you weave. The fear? That without a design
degree or expensive software, your story
might lack the visual punch it deserves. This
is where Mojo's genius shines.

Mojo doesn't just offer templates; it
empowers creators with a palette to paint
their unique stories, leveling the playing field
for all. No longer is exquisite visual
storytelling the domain of those with deep
pockets or specialized training. It's available
to all, and it's rapid. Every swipe, drag, and

drop in Mojo is a step towards breaking the chains that once bound creative expression. Think of Sarah, an amateur travel blogger who had vibrant tales from her journeys but struggled with presenting them visually. Enter Mojo. Using its templates, she transformed her plain photos and clips into mesmerizing stories, drawing thousands to her blog. A simple tool turned her hobby into a lucrative passion, all without breaking the bank.

Section 1.3: The Power of Words: Elevate with Enhanced Captions

The auditory richness of a video is undeniable, but in a world where videos autoplay silently on scrolls, the narrative can often get lost in the mute ambiance. The fear here is straightforward: Your message might drown in the silence. Then, there's the motivation: The quest to make every word, every frame count.

THE CAPTIONs app redefines this narrative. It emphasizes that while videos are visual, their essence often lies in the words they carry. It's not about adding a simple subtitle; it's about enhancing, elaborating, and elevating your content. And while professional transcription might seem out of reach for many, this app ensures top-notch captioning without the accompanying price tag or time drain.

Consider Raj, a deaf entrepreneur who often felt excluded in the digital realm. With THE CAPTIONs app, not only could he consume content more accessibly, but he also started his motivational series, ensuring it was inclusive from the get-go. His series resonated, drawing attention from both the hearing and the deaf community, exemplifying the power of inclusive content.

Section 1.4: The Power of Automation with ChatGPT

The social media landscape is vast and ever-evolving. Every content creator, influencer, or brand often faces a whirlwind of tasks – from ideating content to replying to fans, from scheduling posts to analyzing metrics. The lurking fear is this: In trying to do everything, you might spread yourself too thin. And the motivation is ever-present – the desire to stay relevant, consistent, and impactful without burning out.

Enter the realm of automation, with ChatGPT leading the charge. It's not just about automating tasks; it's about smartly delegating them. By allowing ChatGPT to handle routine queries, draft initial content outlines, or even assist in research, you free up valuable time. Time that can be channeled into creative endeavors, strategic planning, or even some well-deserved rest. No longer are you chasing the clock; you're mastering it.

Imagine Leo, an emerging content strategist who juggled multiple clients. His days were filled with incessant emails, repetitive research, and the pressure of deadlines. Discovering ChatGPT transformed his workflow. He began using it to draft content outlines, answer basic client queries, and even for quick research. As a result, his productivity soared, client satisfaction increased, and he finally had evenings free for himself. Leo's story is a testament to how automation, when used judiciously, can turn the tide in your favor.

I even used ChatGPT to help me organize and create this book (Hint, Hint)

Chapter 2: Future-Proofing: The Evolving Landscape of Social Media

In a digital dance of ceaseless change, knowing the steps isn't enough. It's about being nimble, anticipating the next move, and dancing to the ever-changing rhythm.

Section 2.1: Trends on the Horizon

Social media, at its core, is about engagement. But how we engage, the mediums we use, and even the nature of our interactions, keep evolving. Fears arise from the unknown - the next big trend that might take your brand by surprise. The motivation, though, is the endless opportunity every new trend brings. New audiences, novel content types, and innovative ways to convey your message.

Case Story: **Sarah**, a lifestyle influencer, once remarked, "Five years back, who'd have thought I'd be doing an AR-based makeup tutorial?" That's the magic of the horizon – the uncharted promise it holds.

Subsection 2.1.1: The Rise of Virtual Personalities

As lines blur between reality and virtual, synthesia AI and digital avatars come to the fore. While some might fear this move away from 'authentic' human influencers, others see a realm of possibility. Virtual personalities, unburdened by human constraints, can engage audiences in novel ways, from fantastical narratives to 24/7 interactions. It's a brave new world, with opportunities aplenty for those ready to embrace the shift.

Case Story: **Pixel**, a digital avatar, recently held a 72-hour non-stop Q&A session on a prominent social platform. Fans poured in from across time zones, drawn by the novelty and sheer endurance of this virtual personality. Pixel's creators, a small indie studio, found themselves in a whirlwind of sponsorship deals and collaborations.

Subsection 2.1.2: The Ever-Changing Algorithm

Algorithms: the invisible puppeteers of the digital realm. Content creators often find themselves dancing to its tune, fearing its updates, and constantly seeking to master its whims. But the real challenge isn't understanding today's algorithm; it's about developing a flexible strategy that evolves with it. As the digital sands shift, adaptable content and agile branding can ensure you remain at the forefront.

Case Story: **Mike's Tech Talk**, a YouTube channel, had nailed the algorithm. Consistent views, growing subscribers. But an update halved their viewership overnight. Instead of panicking, Mike surveyed his audience, tweaked his content, and diversified across platforms. Three months later, his audience was more engaged than ever, showcasing the power of adaptability.

Section 2.2: Sustainability in the Digital Age

The desire for viral moments is compelling, but lasting digital success isn't built on transient fame. It's crafted through consistent value, authentic engagement, and a commitment to evolving alongside your audience. This is where the pain point emerges – the daunting task of sustaining in an ephemeral world. But the rewards? A legacy, an evergreen brand, and an engaged, loyal community.

Case Story: **Ella's Vegan Delights** began as an Instagram page sharing vegan recipes. Over time, as food trends ebbed and flowed, Ella focused on community building. She ran interactive polls, collaborated with her followers, and started weekly live-cooking sessions. Today, while many 'trendy' pages have faded, Ella's community thrives, underscoring the essence of digital sustainability.

Chapter 3: Monetizing Your Online Presence

You've poured your heart into your online content. Those sleepless nights fine-tuning a post, that frustration when engagement was low, and the excitement with every new follower. Yet, there's this niggling thought: "How do I turn my passion into profit?" Dive in, let's transform those digital thumbs-ups into real-world banknotes.

Section 3.1: Beyond Ad Revenue

Ad revenue. The go-to dream, right? Those visions of passive income as views skyrocket. But here's some real talk—what if I told you that's just scratching the surface? There's so much more beneath, waiting for you to tap into.

Remember those evenings staring at your screen, wishing those ad dollars were more consistent? Yeah, that unpredictability? We're about to leave it in the dust.

Take Liam's story, for instance. A travel vlogger who saw his ad revenue drop during a season of low viewership. Instead of sulking, he dove deep—into affiliate marketing, brand collabs, and even selling his own merchandise. Now? He's making more than he ever did from ads alone.

Subsection 3.1.1: Affiliate Marketing Magic

You know those products you love and can't stop talking about? What if every time you raved about them online and someone bought them, you got a piece of the pie? That's affiliate marketing for you.

Zoe, with her fitness blog, transformed her genuine recommendations—those yoga mats, energy bars, training shoes—into clickable affiliate links. The result? Every purchase via her links added to her income. No more anxiously waiting for the next paycheck, because with every recommendation, she was crafting her own.

Subsection 3.1.2: Selling Merchandise & Products

You've got a brand, a voice, a community that resonates with your message. Why not wear that pride, literally? Merch isn't just about slapping a logo on stuff—it's about letting your followers carry a piece of what you've built.

Picture this: Jason's podcast, "Geek Chronicles," with its catchy "Stay Geeky" sign-off. A simple phrase now adorns T-shirts, mugs, and caps. His fans? They're

walking billboards of his brand, spreading
the geeky love.

Section 3.2: Leveraging Connections
Ever felt that pang of jealousy seeing others
collaborate or land cool sponsorships? Push
that aside. It's your time now. Because in the
digital world, it's not just about what you
create but the relationships you cultivate.

Subsection 3.2.1: The Power of Sponsorships
Let's get one thing straight: Brands aren't just
looking for faces; they're scouting for voices,
stories, and communities. Your uniqueness is
your pitch. Think beyond the paycheck; think
of the credibility and the doors each
sponsorship can open.

Anna, once a small-scale beauty influencer,
is living proof. A single sponsorship
catapulted her to stardom. The money was
good, sure, but the respect and increased
following? Priceless.

Subsection 3.2.2: Paid Partnerships & Collaborations
Two minds, double the creativity.
Collaborations aren't just about blending
styles—they're about expanding horizons,
both for creators and their audiences.

Clara and Raj, two indie musicians, merged
their worlds in a virtual duet. Their
collaboration? Pure magic. Suddenly, they

weren't just representing their genres, but a fusion that the world hadn't heard before. Their reward? A skyrocketing fanbase and concert deals pouring in.

Chapter 4: Pitching The Game-Changer: ChatGPT

You've probably been there—staring at the blinking cursor, waiting for the words to flow. It's late, your coffee's gone cold, and inspiration is MIA. Enter ChatGPT, not just your average tool, but your creative partner, ready to dive deep with you for just $20 a month. It's the dawn of a new era in content creation, and you're at the forefront.

Section 4.1: Beyond Basic Text

ChatGPT is not just another tool in your digital toolkit—it's a revolution. Picture this: a brainstorming session where you're never alone, and every idea, no matter how wild, gets a sounding board. Feeling that weight of content creation on your shoulders? Let's ease it off.

Subsection 4.1.1: Content Ideas & Brainstorming

Ever had those days when every idea feels overdone, and nothing seems to click? We've all been there. Imagine having a buddy, anytime you need, spitting out fresh content ideas tailored to your vibe.

Meet Sara. She was about to give up her dream of running a sustainable fashion blog, drained of ideas. With ChatGPT, not only did she revive her passion, but her blog flourished with a mix of trending and evergreen topics. From a struggling blogger to a trendsetter, all thanks to a shift in her brainstorming strategy.

Subsection 4.1.2: Brand Refinement & Positioning

In the vast ocean of content, being another fish won't do. You need to be the freaking mermaid. Understanding your unique brand voice and positioning is crucial. Think of ChatGPT as your brand consultant, helping you carve your niche and stand tall.

Remember Jake? His tech reviews were solid but drowned in a sea of similar content. A few sessions with ChatGPT, refining his voice and approach, and boom! He's now the go-to guy for no-nonsense tech breakdowns.

Section 4.2: The Art of Engagement

In the world of social media, every 'like', comment, and share counts. It's not just about broadcasting—it's about conversation. And here's the secret sauce: ChatGPT, making every interaction count.

Subsection 4.2.1: Crafting Captivating Captions

Recall those times when your image was on point, but the words just...lacked? Captions breathe life into content. With ChatGPT, each caption isn't just words—it's a narrative, a story beckoning your audience.

Take Lucy's Instagram. A passionate baker, her delightful cakes were a treat for the eyes, but her captions? Not so appetizing. Once she started crafting stories around her bakes with ChatGPT, her engagement rates baked to perfection.

Subsection 4.2.2: Bio Optimization & First Impressions

Your bio is the gateway to your digital universe. It's the "Hey, come on in!" of the online world. You wouldn't welcome guests into a messy living room, right? Similarly, a crisp, captivating bio can be the difference between a casual scroll-past and a dedicated follower.

Let's talk about Ravi. A passionate travel photographer, his pictures spoke a thousand words, but his bio? Barely a few. Once he optimized it with ChatGPT's insights, not only did his follower count rise, but he also landed partnerships with travel magazines.

Chapter 5: Staying Ahead: Continuous Learning & Adaptation

In the vast expanse of the digital universe, your journey can feel eerily similar to leveling up in an RPG game. Think about it. At the start, you're given basic tools—a wooden sword, maybe. But as you forge ahead, battling demons and acquiring skills, you discover that greater weapons and tools exist. Imagine stumbling upon Thor's Mjölnir in a wooden chest, only to realize you're not yet ready to wield its power. That's the world of AI tools for you. You need the expertise, the 'leveling up', to truly unleash their potential.

Section 5.1: The Importance of Continuous Education

Ah, those late nights where you'd sit, feeling like you've hit a dead end with your content. Where you'd think you're running in circles, trapped in a maze of mediocrity. That changes now. These AI tools? They're like that level 100 weapon, waiting for a master. They aren't just programs; they're potential waiting to be unlocked.

Subsection 5.1.1: Platforms & Tools

Ever looked at a tool, feeling like a basket weaver gazing at Mjölnir? Not knowing the first thing about its power? The digital world is full of these 'Mjölnirs'. Dive into them. Master them. Don't just have the tools; become the craftsman who knows every intricate detail.

Subsection 5.1.2: Adapting to Algorithm Changes

Here's the bitter pill: The algorithm's dance is fickle. One day you're in step, and the next, the rhythm's all changed. But the champions, the influencers who seem to own the game? They're ahead. They anticipate, they move, they shake things up. They don't just react; they reinvent.

Section 5.2: Seeking Inspiration Outside Your Niche

Meet Lara. She was a lifestyle blogger. One day, while watching a documentary on ancient civilizations, she was struck by their beauty routines. She blended those ancient secrets with modern-day products and bam! She had a series that not only went viral but also defined her brand. Lesson? Stop being a fish in your pond. Sometimes, the ocean has the secrets you need.

Now, listen closely. The age-old adage 'Don't reinvent the wheel'? It's gold. Yes, creativity is cherished, but sometimes, it's about looking at the masterpiece wheel and giving it your unique spin. Schools preach against 'copying', but the world? It thrives on inspiration. It's not about duplicating; it's about understanding a blueprint and then, innovating. If you want to reign supreme, sometimes it's about finding a path already paved and strutting down it with your own flair. That's not cheating; that's smart business.

Chapter 6: Networking & Collaboration

"Hey, loved your video. Could I give it a
little twist?"
That was the simple DM that started it all.
From one small comment, my entire social
media strategy transformed. I learned early
on that every post, every comment, and every
share was an opportunity, not just for
exposure, but for collaboration. And let's be
real: in the vast expanse of the digital realm,
you can't—shouldn't—go it alone.

Section 6.1: The Power of Connections
Remember those days where your posts felt
like they were just getting lost in the sea of
content? When you felt like a small fish in an
overwhelmingly large ocean? I've been there.
But a change in perspective turned it all
around. Every interaction, no matter how
minor it seems, can be the bridge to a new
opportunity.

Subsection 6.1.1: Reaching Out to Like-Minded Creators
The journey from one DM to five video
editors from around the globe didn't happen
overnight. These editors, passionate about
their craft and eager to make their mark,
offered their services for a mere $5 a pop.
And here's the thing: these gems are
everywhere. They're not always on Fiverr or
Upwork. They're starting out, just like you
once did. The talent pool is vast. Dive in.

Subsection 6.1.2: Building Mutually Beneficial Relationships

Today, I've got a team. Three content managers and those video editors. Each person, offering a unique skill set, all working harmoniously for a common goal. But this synergy didn't come easy. It took understanding, negotiating, and ensuring that every collaboration was a two-way street. It's not about just taking; it's about giving back in equal measure.

Section 6.2: Handling Outreach

Growth is thrilling. But with it comes its own set of challenges. My inbox? A whirlwind of offers, pitches, and collaboration requests. But here's the deal: Not all opportunities are created equal.

Subsection 6.2.1: Vetting Opportunities

There's a saying that not all that glitters is gold. This couldn't be truer in the digital space. Every offer that lands in your DM isn't your next big break. Some are golden tickets, while others... let's just say they're not worth your time. Learning to discern between the two? Priceless.

Subsection 6.2.2: Establishing Boundaries

You're growing, and that's fantastic. But remember, as much as collaboration is the key, it's crucial to guard your energy. Every 'Yes' shouldn't be automatic. It should be considered, measured against your brand's ethos and values. It's not about being exclusive; it's about being smart.

I can still remember the rush of excitement every time a new message notification popped up. Someone from halfway across the world, appreciating my work, offering their expertise. It was humbling. And it made me realize the boundless opportunities the digital world offered. It's a world where borders blur, where collaboration is the currency, and where the next game-changer could be just a message away. So, go ahead, put yourself out there. Your dream team might just be waiting in the wings.

Chapter 7: Handling Feedback & Trolls

The Matrix Effect of Feedback

Jumping headfirst into the content creation space feels a bit like that iconic scene from *The Matrix* when Neo first wakes up to reality. It's disorienting, stark, and not everyone's going to pat your back. Heck, some days, it'll feel like the matrix downright broke, with even close friends throwing shade. Ever had that gut-wrenching moment when a supposed 'friend' suddenly ghosts or worse, becomes a keyboard warrior against you? I feel you. Those individuals, the ones who were supposed to be in your corner? Time to let them go. Their negativity is the poison to your creativity.

Here's a little secret: there's an almost predictable cycle in the feedback you'll get.

- **Excitement Phase:**
  Oh, the joy of those first few posts.

People cheer, applaud, and support. You'll feel on top of the world.

- **Saturation Point:** Then, the narrative shifts. "Aren't you posting too much?" They'll whisper, sometimes directly, sometimes behind screens. The unfollowers might even start trickling in.
- **Admiration Station:** But hang in there. Because soon after, you'll encounter a different crowd— the ones who'll admire not just your content but your resilience. Your consistency.

Negative comments will sting, but here's your armor against them: "Those who matter don't mind and those who mind don't matter." And when in doubt? Let ChatGPT help you craft that perfect, world-watching response. After all, your platform is not just about your content; it's a testament to your openness to new ideas and growth.

Section 7.1: Constructive Criticism vs. Trolling

Ever felt like each comment, each piece of feedback, is a mini audition? You're always in the spotlight, and everyone's a critic. But it's crucial to differentiate the helpful coaches from the plain hecklers.

Subsection 7.1.1: Embracing Constructive Feedback

Here's a golden nugget: every piece of genuine feedback is a stepping stone to your growth. Instead of shielding yourself from criticism, use it as a compass to refine your path.

Subsection 7.1.2: "Those who mind don't matter, and those who matter don't mind."

Say it with me, let it become your mantra. You're in this for your authentic tribe, not the naysayers. Keep your eyes and energy on the ones lighting up your path.

Section 7.2: Using AI for Handling Feedback

Here's where the game changes. As your audience grows, so does the spectrum of feedback. Navigating this maze can be taxing, but not when you've got ChatGPT by your side. It's like having a seasoned PR manager, but digital, efficient, and always on point.

Subsection 7.2.1: Crafting Thoughtful Responses

Negative feedback can evoke a whirlwind of emotions. But with ChatGPT, you can respond with poise, tact, and grace. Let the world see your maturity, even in the face of harsh critiques.

Subsection 7.2.2: Automating Feedback Management

You've got content to create, dreams to chase. Let AI streamline the feedback process, ensuring every follower feels heard, but without draining your creative energy.

In this vast digital arena, every comment, like, or troll is a reflection of your impact. Wear it as a badge of honor, learn, adapt, and always, always keep shining.

Chapter 8: The Future of Social Media

"Adapt or perish, now as ever, is nature's inexorable imperative." - H.G. Wells. This sentiment holds true for the ever-evolving world of social media. As we chart our way through this digital age, it's not just about

surviving, but thriving in the shifting sands of the online world.

Section 8.1: Emerging Platforms & Trends

Here's the thing about social media trends: by the time everyone's talking about them, the early adopters are already reaping the benefits. Being proactive, rather than reactive, can make all the difference. Think of the possibilities: the next viral platform could be your playground to skyrocket your influence. Want in on a secret? It's often as simple as "copy-paste-success". Seek out what's already working, replicate it, and watch the magic unfold.

Subsection 8.1.1: Platform Diversification

Picture this: investing all your savings in a single stock. Risky, right? The same logic applies to social media. Relying solely on one platform is a gamble. Spread your wings. Use tools like Metricool to efficiently post your short-form content across various platforms, ensuring a broader audience reach and reducing the risk of sudden algorithm changes.

Subsection 8.1.2: Staying Updated

The digital realm is ever-changing. Apps come and go, trends rise and fall. Tools like the Reels app can be game-changers, offering templates to jump on trending content seamlessly. Make it a habit to scour the app stores, read reviews, and always be on the lookout for the next big tool or trend.

Section 8.2: Preparing for the Unpredictable

Dreaming big is great, but without a plan, it remains just that – a dream. The success you see on social media isn't spontaneous; it's the fruit of meticulous planning and consistent effort. Posting consistently, bulk filming, editing, and ensuring there's always content lined up isn't serendipity; it's strategy.

Subsection 8.2.1: The Importance of Flexibility

In the wise words of Gary Vaynerchuk, "Document, don't create." Life is unpredictable, and your content strategy should be adaptable to mirror that. Whether it's a new trend, a personal life change, or an unforeseen global event, the ability to pivot your content strategy can be your superpower.

Subsection 8.2.2: Lifelong Learning

Arguably, one of the most invaluable tools in your arsenal is your capacity to learn. And not just from social media gurus, but from the treasure troves of knowledge packed in books and audiobooks. Commit to absorbing a lifetime of wisdom, one page or one audio chapter at a time. The insights from history, business strategies, or even fictional tales can spark the innovation you need for your next big social media move.

In conclusion, navigating the future of social media isn't about predicting every twist and turn but about being prepared, adaptable, and ever-curious. Buckle up; it's going to be a thrilling ride.

Chapter 9: Monetization & Building a Sustainable Income

Turning passion into a profession isn't just a dream. It's practical. Beyond the glitz of likes and shares on social media lies the real gold: monetization. But here's the catch: every post, every share, every piece of content should be strategically designed to turn a profit.

Action Step: Start by defining your brand and its values. Every content piece should echo these principles.

Section 9.1: Affiliate Marketing & Partnerships

Unlock the power of passive income with affiliate marketing. By partnering with businesses and promoting their products, you earn a commission for each sale made through your unique link. ClickBank, for instance, boasts of partnerships with over 6 million vendors globally.

Action Step: Register on platforms like ClickBank, Amazon Associates, or ShareASale to explore products that fit your brand.

Subsection 9.1.1: Identifying the Right Affiliates

Selecting the right partners is key. Not all products will resonate with your audience.

The best influencers select products they genuinely love and believe in.

Action Step: Research and list down ten products you love and think will be a hit with your audience. Approach these companies for partnership.

Subsection 9.1.2: Ethical Promotion

Never, ever promote something you don't trust. Your followers rely on your word. Make it count.

Action Step: Always test a product before promoting it. If it's not something you'd personally use, think twice before endorsing.

Section 9.2: Merchandising & Product Launches

Your brand is more than just digital. Translate it into tangible products that your audience can buy.

Action Step: Survey your audience. Discover what products they'd love to buy from you. Is it a T-shirt? An eBook? A course?

Subsection 9.2.1: Designing with Your Audience in Mind

Create products that your audience craves. Understand their needs, preferences, and desires.

Action Step: Use tools like SurveyMonkey or Google Forms to understand what your followers want.

Subsection 9.2.2: Launch Strategies
Master the art of a launch. Timing, marketing, and promotion play a huge role in a product's success.

Action Step: Dive into "Launch" by Jeff Walker. It's a step-by-step guide on effective product launches.

Section 9.3: Premium Content & Subscription Models
Exclusive content can be a steady revenue source. Platforms like Patreon and OnlyFans allow creators to offer premium content at a fee.

Action Step: Begin with one exclusive content piece a month. Monitor the traction it gains and adjust your strategy.

Subsection 9.3.1: Choosing the Right Model
Different platforms cater to different audiences. Understand where your audience resides and target that platform.

Action Step: Conduct an audience audit. Are they more likely to use Patreon or OnlyFans? Make an informed decision.

Subsection 9.3.2: Delivering Value

Ensure that your premium content is exceptional. Quality over quantity, always.

Action Step: Collaborate with experts in your niche to co-create content. This way, you offer unparalleled value to your subscribers.

With these strategies and action steps, the path to monetization becomes less daunting and more achievable. The ball is now in your court. Implement, iterate, and witness your digital empire

Grow.

Chapter 10: The Long Game: Building a Legacy with Digital Entrepreneurship

The digital realm might seem ephemeral to some. Posts disappear in 24 hours, trends fade, and the next shiny thing is always around the corner. But here's the deal: the digital world is far more profound than one might think. It's not just about today; it's about shaping tomorrow. And for those on the fence about social media, consider this - it's not just a hobby; it's a gateway to tools and opportunities that are simply groundbreaking.

The Stadium Effect:

You know, I didn't always view social media with such clarity. My true "a-ha" moment came at a Keller Williams seminar. Imagine this: every time between 1,000 to 10,000 people view your content, that's like filling a stadium. A *stadium*, people! That's the power of reach we're talking about, and the influence one can wield.

The Beauty of Globalization:
Then there was this time I felt overwhelmed with video editing. I mean, the sheer thought of it was exhausting. But out of the blue, I started getting DMs with folks offering to edit my videos. I threw out a number, "$5", expecting a laugh or counter-offer. Instead, I was met with an agreement. It's astonishing how value varies across countries. My friend once shelled out $500 for a short video, and here I was, leveraging the power of apps like Mojo and the global marketplace, creating content for peanuts. It wasn't just about the savings; it was the revelation: with the right tools and approach, this social media game? It's a walk in the park.

From Inspiration to Creation:
Books have always been my backbone. *The Laptop Millionaire*, for instance, was a spontaneous find during a random Google search. Little did I know, that very book would sow the seeds for this one you're reading now. Sometimes, destiny hides in the simplest of searches.

Using AI Tools:
And, let's not forget tools like Opus.pro.
Time crunch? Editors lagging behind? I'd just
take long footage, churn out short,
compelling content, ranked from best to
worst. We're living in an age where AI
doesn't just assist; it excels!

Pushing Past Doubt:
Starting out? I won't sugarcoat it: it was
paralyzing. The self-doubt was real. But time
has this magic of thinning out the crowd. The
longer you stay in the game, the more you
realize that the haters? They're just
background noise. One pivotal shift for me
was when I began receiving calls for advice.
It dawned on me - I needed to start taking my
own advice. You see, sometimes we're blind
to our potential, but crystal clear about
others'. And if there's one mantra I abide by,
it's this: "Those who matter don't mind, and
those who mind don't matter." Surround
yourself with growers, builders, creators.
Learn from those who've walked the path.
And remember, anyone throwing shade is
probably stagnating in their own shadows.

In Summation:
This journey, and this book, isn't born from
thin air. It's a rich tapestry of ideas, insights,

and learnings from countless books, audiobooks, and lived experiences. So, as you flip these pages, know that you're not just reading a book; you're accessing a legacy of knowledge.

Conclusion: Your Digital Toolkit Unveiled

And so, dear reader, we come to the end of our journey together, one that has been an exhilarating ride of insights, breakthroughs, and transformation. But before we part ways, let's distill everything into a crystal-clear action plan for the seasoned digital entrepreneurs who might want just the bare essentials.

- **Embrace AI**: Start with **GPTE.ai**. Think of it as your personal digital warehouse, brimming with AI tools. Why search everywhere when everything's in one place?
- **Unleash the Power of Thought**: **ChatGPT** is not just a tool; it's a game-changer. It'll shape and refine your thoughts, opening doors to creative vistas you'd never imagined.
- **Visual Storytelling**: With **Synthesia.Ai**, you've got the power of avatars. SOPs, ads, explainer videos, you name it, it's got it.
- **Voice Magic**: **Play.ht** transforms written scripts into impeccable voiceovers. No more stumbling over words or costly studio time.
- **Video Crafting**: Use **Opus.pro** to transform extensive content into engaging short clips. Partner it with **the captions app** to ensure every word gets seen, and the **mojo app** to infuse raw footage with style and aesthetics.
- **Execution Blueprint**: The essence of this book? It's a toolkit. And with this toolkit, your social media career is set to thrive.

The principle? Post more to gain more. Use Canva to craft appealing ads post on instagram, Facebook, snapchat, tiktok and wait for the video editors content managers and other help flow in (this may take upwards to a month make sure you're posting consistent content). For just about $50 a month, delegate to a dedicated social media content manager. They'll optimize and distribute across platforms. Your job? Keep filming those raw moments of brilliance.

The heart of the matter is this: Starting is everything. Once you do, the universe conspires to place every tool you need right into your hands. With just a smartphone, you have an entire world of opportunities awaiting you.

Thank you for being part of this journey. It's my sincere hope that every page of this book has chipped away at any barriers, doubts, or hesitations you might've had. You're equipped, you're ready, and the digital space eagerly awaits your mastery.

If the road ahead throws you a curveball or if you're just hungry for more insights, I'm here. Find me across the digital realm @williamtstewart. I look forward to our paths crossing, our conversations, and the shared joy of digital innovation. Good luck, and till we meet again!

Bonus Chapter: Building My Media Dream Team with AI & Vision

We often hear the phrase, "It takes a village." Well, in the world of media creation, it could be rephrased as, "It takes a team." But building that team doesn't have to mean hiring a whole crew of full-time employees with sky-high salaries. With the right approach, innovative tools, and a clear vision, I built a dynamic media team that brought my brand to life.

The Idea and The Vision:

My journey began with a simple idea: I needed a team. But not just any team. I wanted a team that understood my vision, ethos, and what I wanted to achieve. The foundational step was to map out what this team would look like. For this, I turned to an AI assistant - ChatGPT. With its help, I meticulously wrote out the roles, responsibilities, and interactions of each team member.

The Roles:

- **Content Strategist:** This role was pivotal. The content strategist is responsible for posting all content, curating the content calendar, brainstorming content ideas, and tracking video creation. In essence, this person is the beating heart of my content pipeline.
- **Videographers:** With my foothold in real estate, one videographer specializes in listing photos, while another focuses on

videography. Their output is essential, and their creations flow into a shared Dropbox.

- **Video Editors:** After videographers do their magic, the content goes to editors. Describing my vision for each edit was made easier with ChatGPT, ensuring my content always aligns with my brand's tone and message.
- **Graphic Designer:** A brand's visual identity can make or break its image. My graphic designer oversees website design and ensures a consistent visual branding across platforms.

The Planning Phase:

This phase was all about documentation. I crafted extensive Word documents and a brand outline. This wasn't just a mere task; it was an intricate process that required thought, clarity, and precision. To demonstrate the depth of this endeavor, I've enclosed that very document for you, showcasing the meticulous work and dedication poured into creating my media team.

Reaching Out:

With my brand document at the ready, I ventured out to recruit new editors. This document wasn't just a brief; it was a testament to my brand's essence, capturing its spirit, purpose, and goals.

SOPs and Financial Planning:
Standard Operating Procedures (SOPs) are crucial. It's like a playbook for your team, ensuring everyone is on the same page. Again, ChatGPT was invaluable in helping create these. Moreover, it assisted in devising a financial plan, ensuring every team member was rewarded fairly, not just with monetary compensation but also with the shared vision of our collective growth.

The Power of Sweat Equity:
What made my team special was our shared vision. Every team member is invested in the brand's growth, contributing high-quality work because they believe in what we're building together.

Conclusion:
Building a media team is an intricate dance of planning, vision, and execution. But with the right tools, especially AI, and a shared goal, it's possible to build a dream team without breaking the bank. This chapter isn't just about sharing my journey; it's an invitation to think big, plan carefully, and use technology to your advantage.

And as promised, here's my brand document as a bonus. Dive in, be inspired, and remember – the sky's the limit!

[Insert Brand Document]

Remember, every monumental structure started with a blueprint. Consider this chapter yours. Happy building!

AI TOOLS HONORABLE MENTIONS:

Durable.co Create websites instantly
Aivalley.ai a list of ai tools
Beautiful.ai create presentations with simple sentences